First Facts

Faceless, Spineless, and Brainless Ocean Animals

SEA CUCUMBERS

by Jody S. Rake

Consultant:
Dr. Deborah Donovan
Professor, Biology Department and Science Education Group
Western Washington University
Bellingham, Washington

CAPSTONE PRESS
a capstone imprint

First Facts are published by Capstone Press,
1710 Roe Crest Drive, North Mankato, Minnesota 56003
www.mycapstone.com

Library of Congress Cataloging-in-Publication Data
Names: Rake, Jody Sullivan, author.
Title: Sea cucumbers / by Jody S. Rake.
Description: North Mankato, Minnesota : Capstone Press, [2017] | Series: First facts. Brainless, spineless, and faceless ocean animals | Audience: Ages 7-9._ | Audience: K to grade 3._ | Includes bibliographical references and index. | Description based on print version record and CIP data provided by publisher; resource not viewed.
Identifiers: LCCN 2016001227 (print) | LCCN 2015051439 (ebook) | ISBN 9781515721482 (eBook PDF) | ISBN 9781515721406 (hardcover) | ISBN 9781515721444 (pbk.)
Subjects: LCSH: Sea cucumbers—Juvenile literature. | Marine animals—Juvenile literature.
Classification: LCC QL384.H7 (print) | LCC QL384.H7 R35 2017 (ebook) | DDC 593.9/6—dc23
LC record available at http://lccn.loc.gov/2016001227

Editorial Credits
Abby Colich, editor; Bobbie Nuytten, designer; Kelly Garvin, media researcher; Steve Walker, production specialist

Photo Credits
Corbis/David Fleetham/Visuals Unlimited, 8; Minden Pictures: D.P. Wilson/FLPA, 15, David Shale/NPL, 21, Franco Banfi, 14, Fred Bavendam, 20, Georgette Douwma/NPL, 10, Norbert Wu, 16, Pete Oxford, 11; Seapics/Marc Chamberlain, 9; Shutterstock: Andrea Izzotti, 13, Armin Voeller, 17, Boris Pamikov, 7, e2dan, cover, 1, 19, orlandin, 5

Artistic Elements:
Shutterstock: Artishok, Vikasuh

Printed and bound in China

PO007692RRDF16

Table of Contents

No Backbones

Have you ever seen an animal without a backbone? Many creatures in the sea don't have a backbone. Animals without a backbone, or spine, are **invertebrates**. Sea cucumbers are invertebrates. They have no brain, eyes, or ears, either. Other body parts help them move and find food.

invertebrate—an animal without a backbone

Slug of the Sea

Sea cucumbers have soft, tube-shaped bodies. Most of them look like big worms or slugs.

This animal can be many sizes. Some are less than 1 inch (2.5 centimeters) long. The longest can grow to 6 feet (1.8 meters).

Sea cucumbers live in all the world's oceans. Some live in warm, shallow water near **coral reefs** or the shore. Others live in deeper, darker water.

coral reef—a part of the seafloor made up of the hardened bodies of corals; corals are small, colorful sea creatures

Fact! Scientists have found sea cucumbers near the bottom of the Marianas Trench. The Marianas Trench is the deepest known part of the ocean.

Crawling on Tube Feet

A sea cucumber doesn't have legs. Instead, five rows of tube feet run along its body. Tube feet look like tiny noodles. They work like suction cups. Tube feet stick to the seafloor. Then they let go as the creature moves. Some sea cucumbers get **oxygen** through their tube feet.

tube feet

Different Sea Cucumbers

There are more than 1,200 **species** of sea cucumbers. Most are brightly colored. Some have spots or stripes. Others look fuzzy. The fuzz is actually tube feet. Some sea cucumbers look spiny, but the spines are soft and fleshy.

oxygen—a colorless gas that living things need to survive
species—a group of creatures that are capable of reproducing with one another

What's For Lunch?

Sea cucumbers eat tiny bits of **algae** and **plankton**. They also dine on leftovers from other animals. Sea cucumbers even eat fish poop! They gather food bits with tentacles around their mouths. The tentacles look like tiny tree branches. Waste comes out the other end of their bodies.

Fact! Some sea cucumbers **burrow** into the seafloor for protection. Only their mouth tentacles stick out to collect food.

tentacle

tentacles

mouth

algae—small, plantlike organisms without roots or
    stems that grow in water or on damp surfaces
plankton—tiny organisms that drift in the sea
burrow—to dig a hole in the ground

A Body without a Brain

Sea cucumbers don't have a brain. Instead, they have a system of **nerves**. Five rows of nerves run down the length of the body. Nerves around the mouth help them collect food. Nerves in the skin help the animal sense light.

> **nerve**—a thin strand in the body that carries messages

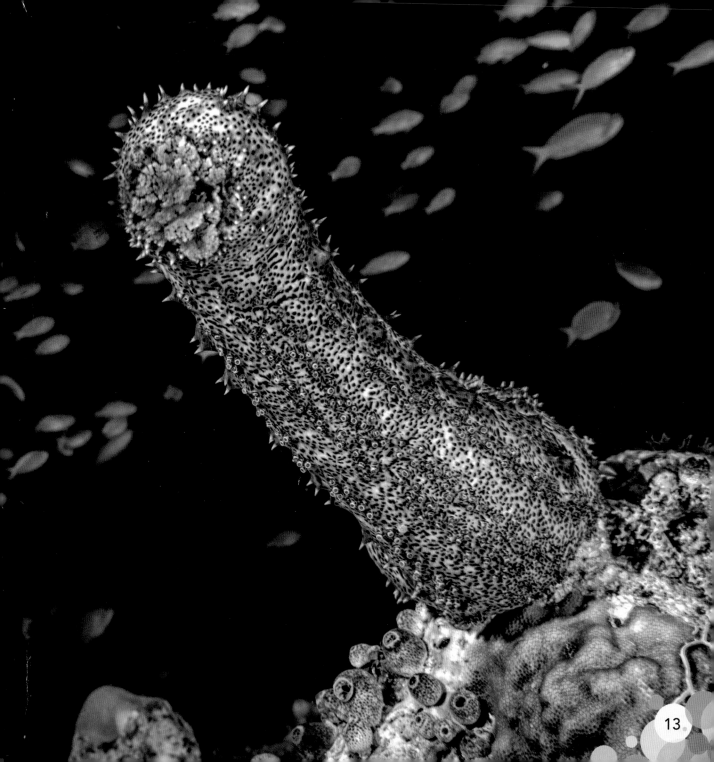

Sea Cucumber Life Cycle

Sea cucumbers **reproduce** by releasing eggs and sperm in the water. The eggs and sperm meet. They soon grow into **larvae**. The floating larvae sink to the seafloor. There they slowly grow. Most species grow into adults in a few years.

reproduce—to make young
larva—a stage of development between egg and adult

Fact! Rarely, sea cucumbers reproduce by regeneration. If a sea cucumber is cut in half, a new animal grows from each half.

larva

Protection for Easy Prey

Many animals eat sea cucumbers. Fish, sea turtles, and sea stars feast on them. Sea cucumbers' slow-moving, squishy bodies make them easy targets. But sea cucumbers have ways to protect themselves. Some burrow into the seafloor. Others release poison. Some species can hide by blending in with their surroundings.

People and Sea Cucumbers

People have uses for sea cucumbers. In some parts of the world, people eat this animal. Fishing for sea cucumbers is called trepanging.

Scientists are studying these creatures. Sea cucumbers may be able to help people who have cancer. They could also help people who have pain in their joints.

Amazing But True!

One sea cucumber defense is truly amazing. When threatened, it can shoot some of its insides out its anus. The predator gets tangled in the sticky organs. This gives the sea cucumber time to escape. The sea cucumber's organs quickly grow back.

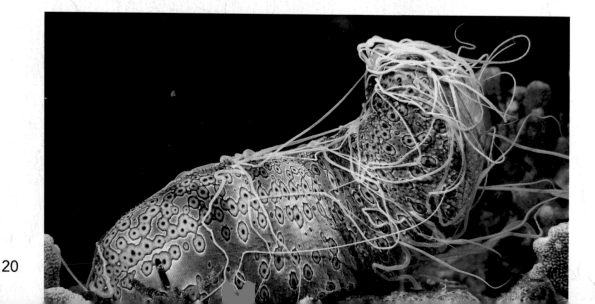

Sea Cucumber Facts

Where it lives: oceans worldwide

Habitat: seafloor

Size: 0.75 inch (2 cm) to 6.5 feet (2 m) long

Diet: algae, plankton, leftovers and waste of other animals

Predators: fish, sea turtles, sea stars

Life span: 5 to 10 years

Status: stable (not at risk of dying out)

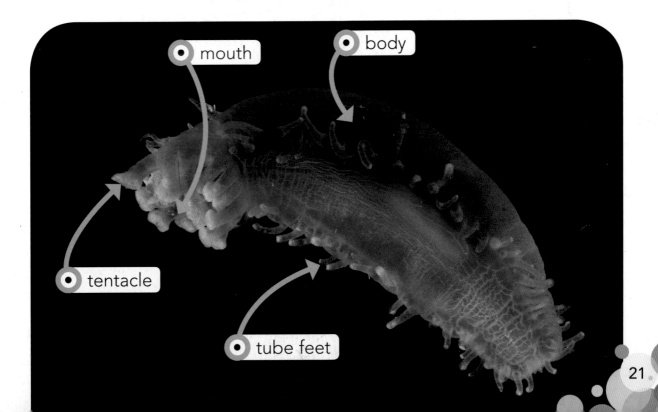

mouth

body

tentacle

tube feet

Glossary

algae (AL-jee)—small, plantlike organisms without roots or stems that grow in water or on damp surfaces

burrow (BUHR-oh)—to dig a hole in the ground

coral reef (KOR-uhl REEF)—a part of the seafloor made up of the hardened bodies of corals; corals are small, colorful sea creatures

invertebrate (in-VUR-tuh-bruht)—an animal without a backbone

larva (LAR-vuh)—a stage of development between egg and adult

nerve (NURV)—a thin strand in the body that carries messages

oxygen (OK-suh-juhn)—a colorless gas that living things need to survive

plankton (PLANGK-tuhn)—tiny organisms that drift in the sea

reproduce (ree-pruh-DOOSE)—to make young

species (SPEE-sheez)—a group of creatures that are capable of reproducing with one another

Read More

Claybourne, Anna, Anita Ganeri and Mike Unwin. *My First Animal Encyclopedia*. New York: Sandy Creek, 2015.

Owen, Ruth. *Disgusting Animal Defenses*. It's a Fact: Real-Life Reads. Cornwall, England: Ruby Tuesday Books, 2014.

Patkau, Karen. *Who Needs a Reef? A Coral Reef Ecosystem*. Plattsburgh, N.Y.: Tundra Books of Northern New York, 2014.

Internet Sites

FactHound offers a safe, fun way to find Internet sites related to this book. All of the sites on FactHound have been researched by our staff.

Here's all you do:

Visit *www.facthound.com*

Type in this code: 9781515721406

Check out projects, games and lots more at
www.capstonekids.com

Critical Thinking Using the Common Core

1. Name a sea cucumber body part and describe how it helps the animal survive. (Key Idea and Details)

2. Reread the text on page 9 and study the photo. Then study another photo of a sea cucumber in the book. Describe how they are different. Then describe what likenesses they have that make them both sea cucumbers. (Craft and Structure)

3. Reread page 8. What if sea cucumbers had legs instead of tube feet? What's one way they might live differently? (Integration of Knowledge and Ideas)

Index